Staff Paper

FOREWORD

The Real Book Staff Paper is the answer to manuscript paper. It is the alternative to the plethora of poorly-designed, no writing-space paper abound on the market. The Real Book Staff Paper has been professionally printed and bound, and the pages are designed to allow plenty of room for notes, ledger lines, text, and other musical notation. Every effort has been made to make it enjoyable to use.

ISBN 978-1-4234-4134-2

HAL•LEONARD®
CORPORATION
7777 W. BLUEMOUND RD. P.O. BOX 13819 MILWAUKEE, WI 53213

Visit Hal Leonard Online at
www.halleonard.com

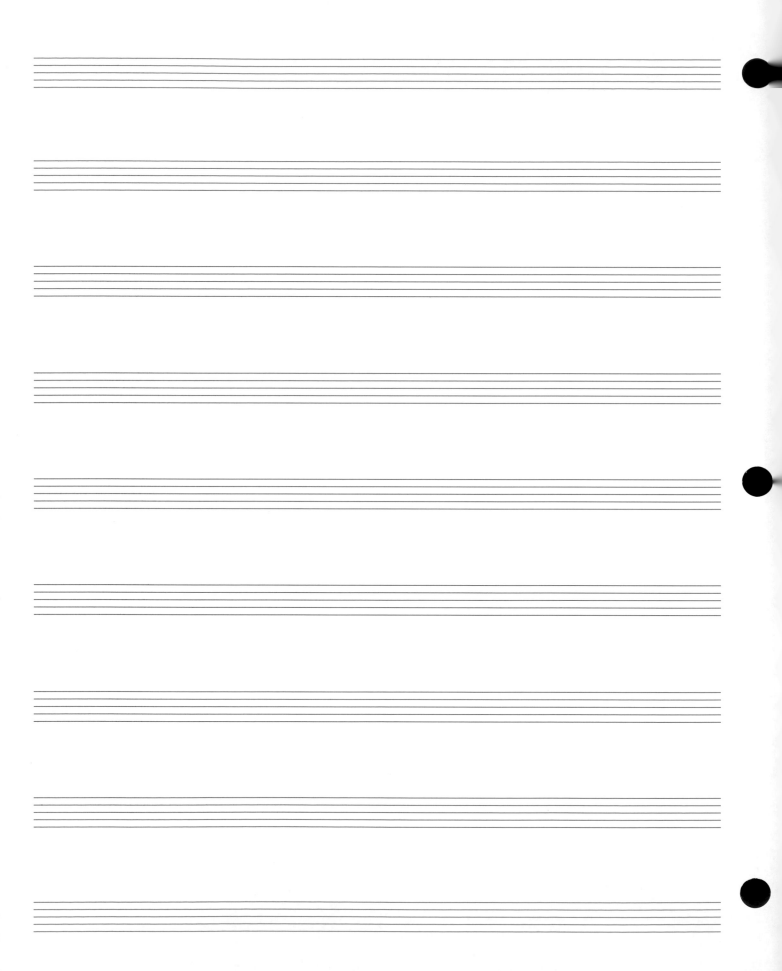